Williamson **W** Publishing

DRAWING HORSES
(that look real!)

Don Mayne

Quick Starts for Kids!

WILLIAMSON PUBLISHING • CHARLOTTE, VERMONT

Library of Congress Cataloging-in-Publication Data

2002027015
Additional Library of Congress Cataloging-in-Publication Data is being processed.

Quick Starts for Kids!™ series editor: **Susan Williamson**
Interior design: **Dana Pierson**
Interior illustrations: **Don Mayne**
Cover design: **Marie Ferrante-Doyle**
Cover illustrations: **horse, Don Mayne; girl, Michael Kline**
Printing: **Capital City Press**

Williamson Publishing Co.
P.O. Box 185
Charlotte, VT 05445
(800) 234-8791

Manufactured in the United States of America

10 9 8 7 6 5 4 3 2 1

Kids Can!®, *Little Hands*®, *Kaleidoscope Kids*®, and *Tales Alive!*®
are registered trademarks of Williamson Publishing.

Good Times™, *Quick Starts for Kids!*™, *Quick Starts Tips!*™, *Quick
Starts Jump-Starts*™, and *You Can Do It!*™ are trademarks of
Williamson Publishing.

Notice: The information contained in this book is true, complete,
and accurate to the best of our knowledge. All recommendations
and suggestions are made without any guarantees on the part of
the author or Williamson Publishing. The author and publisher
disclaim all liability incurred in conjunction with the use of this
information.

Dedication
In memory of my mother,
Barbara Mayne, whose love for
animals inspired me to observe,
cherish, and render them with
affection by seeing with my
heart instead of just my eyes.

Acknowledgments
This book could not be possible
without the enthusiastic con-
tributions of two special horse
lovers, Meredith Baker and
Kalcy O'Keefe. Also, many
thanks to the staff at
Williamson Publishing,
especially Vicky Congdon and
Susan Williamson, for their
encouragement and direction.

If you like to draw, you may enjoy
Don Mayne's other book, published by
Williamson Publishing:

DRAW YOUR OWN CARTOONS!

Winner of an
Oppenheim Toy Portfolio Gold Award

Contents

Yes, You Can Draw Horses!

If you've ever tried to draw a horse but wound up frustrated instead, then this book is for you. *You* can draw horses that look real using my technique, which I'm pleased to share with you. The secrets that people of all ages love to learn about in my art classes can help you learn to draw horses quickly, accurately — and best of all — with hours of enjoyment and satisfaction! If you follow along with me in this book, I can help you, too.

All of the books I've ever seen about drawing horses are full of beautiful pictures that would look great hanging in an art museum. What those books don't seem to show is how *you* can start with a blank piece of paper and end up with something that looks like a horse.

I thought about all the people who just want to learn how to draw a simple picture of a horse so that it looks like a *real* horse — and not like a dog or some other animal. And I decided to share some of the secrets and shortcuts I've learned.

Later on, if you practice drawing and maybe take some art classes, you might be ready to try some "museum quality" horse drawings. You and I will both be very pleased if that happens. But learning to draw horses is a lot like learning to ride them — you have to trot before you can gallop. And this book is all you need to get started!

Don Mayne

chapter 1

The Secrets of Horse-Drawing Success

Here we'll start with the basics — basic supplies, basic shapes, and a very basic (but classic) horse pose. You'll build on the secrets and techniques you learn here in subsequent chapters to fine-tune your drawings and to try more complicated positions and scenes (you can also apply them to drawing other things!). Now, I do have to say this at least once: Drawing real-looking horses takes practice, but practicing is lots of fun. And with my methods, you'll be happy with the results right away!

"STRAIGHT FROM THE HORSE'S MOUTH"

A Stable of Materials

Good news! Drawing horses doesn't cost anywhere near as much as feeding them! These simple supplies can be picked up at any art- or office-supply store:

Pencils. Dixon Ticonderoga #2 pencils are my favorites because they sharpen easily and draw nice, clean lines. But whatever brand you use, be sure the pencil has a clean eraser that really works so you can easily make small, quick corrections while sketching. And keep that point good and sharp!

Black felt- or plastic-tip pens and markers. You'll have lots of choices here, and you'll quickly develop some favorites. It's easiest to work with fine-point permanent black-ink pens (as long as they aren't smelly). You also don't want the ink to *bleed* (spread) into the paper. It's nice to have different-sized tips to make lines of varying thicknesses. If you can,

try out the pens in the store before you buy them. You can easily make corrections to your final inked drawing with correction fluid (page 13).

A large eraser. I couldn't do a finished drawing without one of these! Your eraser must be able to clean up all the pencil marks without leaving any marks of its own. A pink eraser usually works well, but the best kind are the kneaded rubber ones, because they don't leave any "crumbs" behind.

Paper. For practice sketches, you can recycle paper by using the back side of a used sheet. A good-quality drawing paper or *card stock* (a thicker paper that won't wrinkle as easily when you erase) is perfect for your final drawing. For a very special final drawing, try *illustration board* (it's thick and very stiff); you'll probably need to cut it into smaller pieces.

Colored pencils. The more you spend on these, the better the quality and the more colorful they will be. Keep them sharp. At art-supply stores, you can usually buy just the colors you use most often.

"Build" Your Horse with Basic Shapes

Just about anything can be drawn more easily by using basic geometric shapes to "build" the object you're drawing. For drawing horses, this is especially true, because when you "look" inside a horse, it's easy to see that it is made out of distinct shapes. If you sketch these shapes lightly with a pencil first, you will find that your finished drawing looks a lot more like you wanted it to!

Here's an overview of how you build a horse from basic shapes.

We'll look at each step more closely when we draw a horse in its classic pose (pages 16–18).

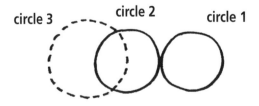

circle 3   circle 2   circle 1

For the body, draw two same-size circles that touch at the edge. Then draw a third, slightly larger, circle that overlaps about halfway into the middle circle.

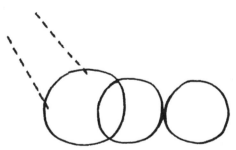

From the larger circle (the front of the horse), draw two straight lines for the neck. They should be slightly closer together at the top.

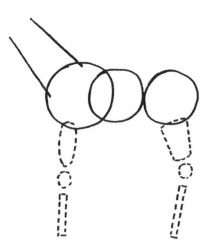  

The front and back legs are a series of ovals, circles, "cup" shapes, and skinny rectangles (leave a little space between them).

The head, like the body, is also made of two circles that are joined together. The ears and hooves are just small triangles.

Now sketch in the remaining parts of the body and add a few details. Do you see how these simple shapes are used to build a horse's body?

Practice Visualizing the Shapes

Visualizing is a very useful way to learn what shapes are hidden inside a horse. Here is an exercise that you can practice over and over to help you identify the shapes that create a horse's basic structure. It works best with horses in *profile* (seen from the side).

1. First, trace just the outline of a horse from a book or a magazine. Be sure to hold the paper very still.

2. Next, see what basic shapes you can fit into the outline, and study how the shapes relate to one another.

SECRET #2

Learn to "R" "I" "D" "E"

The *R.I.D.E. technique* is a secret method that I have developed over many years of teaching drawing. In my classes, I discovered that people aren't afraid to draw, but they *are* afraid to make mistakes. Well, when you use my special R.I.D.E. technique, you can forget about making mistakes, because they don't matter! In fact, with this super-easy method, you can actually use your so-called mistakes to improve your drawing!

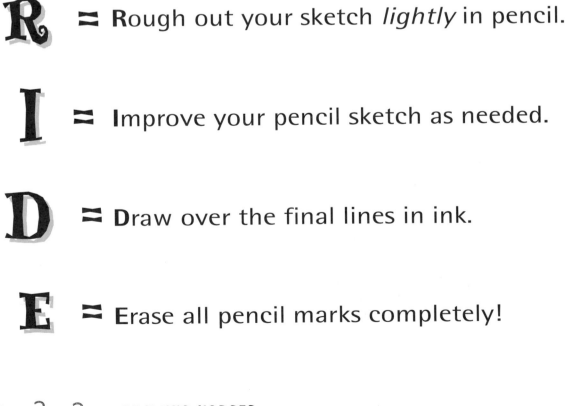

R = Rough out your sketch *lightly* in pencil.

I = Improve your pencil sketch as needed.

D = Draw over the final lines in ink.

E = Erase all pencil marks completely!

DRAWING HORSES

Thumbnail Sketches

Before you spend a lot of time on a drawing, it's always a good idea to plan it first
using a *thumbnail sketch*. This means
starting with a *quick* sketch of the major
basic shapes in your picture on a piece of
scrap paper, so you can see exactly how
it needs to fit on the paper.

Oops!

Thumbnail sketching is especially handy if you want to include things that overlap in
your drawing, like a mare and a foal (pages 48–49), or when you get into more involved
drawings with backgrounds and scenery (pages 58–61). Just a few seconds of thumbnail
sketching can save hours of extra work, so it's a good habit to get into, right from the
start!

Start with a thumbnail sketch.

Start real drawing here.

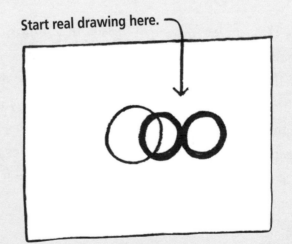

**When you do your real drawing, the
position of the circles of the horse's body
will be your guide to where you should
begin sketching.**

Let's draw a picture of a horse using the **R.I.D.E.** technique. If you follow all the instructions and take your time, you'll be surprised at what a nice drawing you're already able to make! And we haven't even learned the 10 STEPS TO THE CLASSIC HORSE-STATUE POSE (pages 16–18) yet!

Rough out a drawing in pencil, showing the basic shapes of the horse. Because this is just a rough sketch, if you want to start all over with a fresh piece of paper, it's easy to do. Take your time, and get all those shapes in the right places!

Improve your rough sketch by adding details. You can erase and redraw the details to get just the look you want. Don't worry about erasing lines to make the sketch look neat, because you will erase all the pencil marks later anyway. Avoid the temptation to make the pencil lines darker when you redraw them — keep it light!

Draw over the pencil lines with your ink pen as if you were tracing them. Notice in the example that some of the sketched pencil lines don't get drawn in ink (the dotted lines).

It's really important to take your time when you draw in ink. Look carefully at your pencil sketch and pick up your pen from time to time so you know exactly where the lines are going. If you make a mistake in ink, don't worry, because it can be fixed (see page 13).

Erase all the pencil marks carefully after the ink dries (which usually happens quickly). You should hold the paper down firmly on the table to avoid crumpling it. Use a smaller eraser (like the one on your pencil) to rub out any stubborn marks. After the pencil marks are gone, your drawing will look as if it had been finished without any effort at all!

  **DRAWING HORSES**

SECRET #3

There Is No Such Thing as a Mistake When You Are Learning to Draw!

I know that it can be frustrating when you try to draw something that looks real, but the legs turn out too short, or the head too big, or the body too fat.

Well, I've got news for you! Those were not mistakes. They were all opportunities to learn something. If you can see that the legs are too short, for example, then next time you'll sketch them a little longer. See? You learned something!

I always ask my students not to throw away the drawings that they don't like. You don't need to show them to anybody, but it's very helpful to spread them out on the table and draw new pictures right next to them. By doing this, you'll be able to learn from the things you didn't like instead of just being frustrated by them.

And remember, if you really like something you drew, then it doesn't matter at all what anybody else thinks of it. Drawing to please yourself is the most fun of all!

🪢 Quick Starts Tips!™

Correction fluid to the rescue! If you make a mistake with the ink pen, don't panic! Just leave it there, and finish the rest of your drawing. After you have erased all the pencil marks, you can use a nontoxic correction fluid (Like Liquid Paper or Wite-Out) to fix the ink line. Smoothly apply just enough fluid to cover the line that you want to correct. Then — this is important! — let the fluid dry thoroughly. Carefully draw a new ink line right over the "patch."

Observing the Horse

SHAPES

To learn how to draw a horse that *looks* like a horse, you need to practice — well — *looking* at horses! Let's look at this picture together, and I'll point out some observations about a horse's inner shapes and sizes. If you keep these in mind while you sketch, you'll immediately improve your horse drawing.

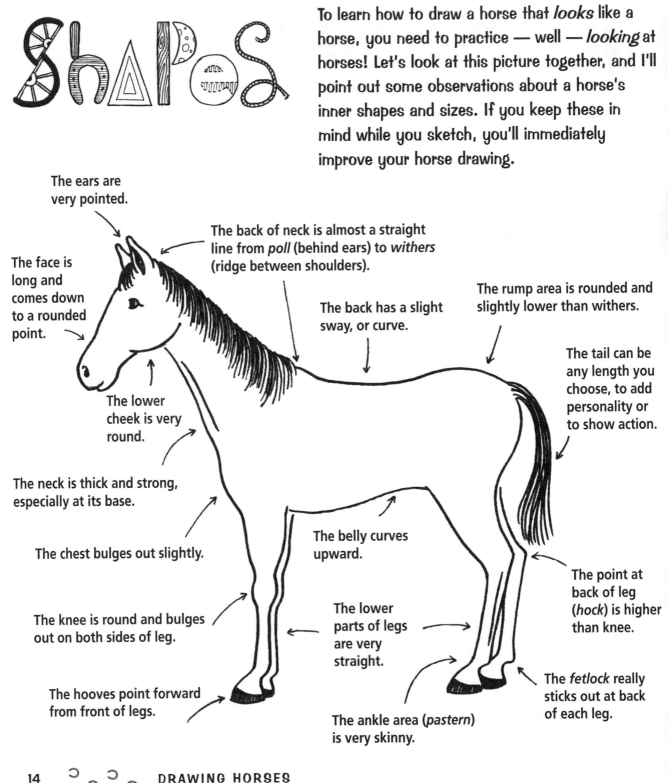

The ears are very pointed.

The face is long and comes down to a rounded point.

The back of neck is almost a straight line from *poll* (behind ears) to *withers* (ridge between shoulders).

The back has a slight sway, or curve.

The rump area is rounded and slightly lower than withers.

The tail can be any length you choose, to add personality or to show action.

The lower cheek is very round.

The neck is thick and strong, especially at its base.

The chest bulges out slightly.

The belly curves upward.

The point at back of leg (*hock*) is higher than knee.

The knee is round and bulges out on both sides of leg.

The lower parts of legs are very straight.

The hooves point forward from front of legs.

The ankle area (*pastern*) is very skinny.

The *fetlock* really sticks out at back of each leg.

PROPORTION

Now we need to look at the proportions of the horse's body. *Proportion* is the relationship between the size of objects. How long are the legs compared with the length of the body? How long should the neck be? To figure out the correct proportions, you can use what I call the *key distance*, the distance between the circles used to sketch the body (page 8). This is the single most important thing you can do to make your drawing look realistic.

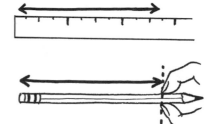

You can measure the key distance by using a ruler or by using your fingers and a pencil.

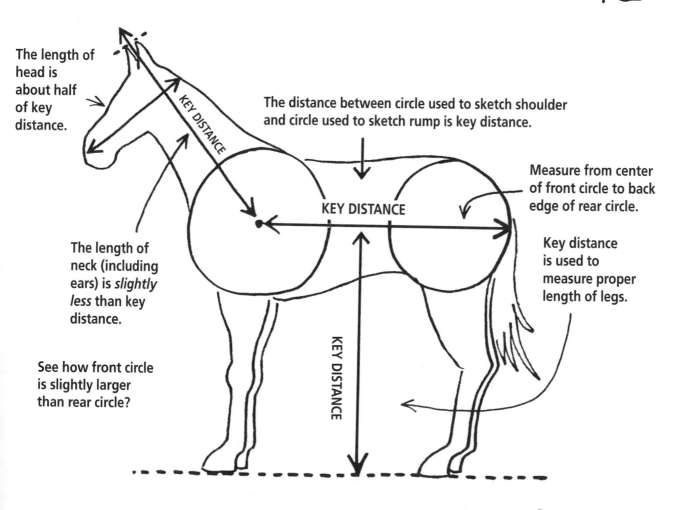

The length of head is about half of key distance.

The length of neck (including ears) is *slightly less* than key distance.

See how front circle is slightly larger than rear circle?

KEY DISTANCE

The distance between circle used to sketch shoulder and circle used to sketch rump is key distance.

KEY DISTANCE

Measure from center of front circle to back edge of rear circle.

Key distance is used to measure proper length of legs.

KEY DISTANCE

10 Steps to the Classic Horse-Statue Pose

OK, here we go! Now we're going to put all of this — basic shapes (pages 8–9), proportion (page 15), and our R.I.D.E. technique (pages 10–12) — together and go step-by-step through the process of drawing a horse. Horse statues and models are typically displayed showing the horse from the side because that pose shows all the details of that particular breed. These instructions will show you how to draw this basic pose very well. Later, you can apply these same techniques to more advanced poses.

   Remember to press lightly with the pencil so you can erase it easily later!

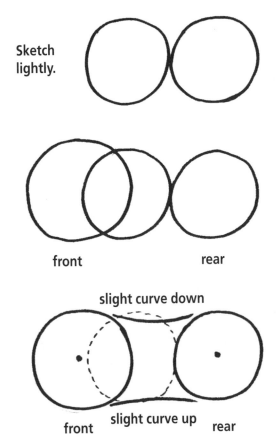

1. Lightly sketch two same-sized circles that just touch at the edge.

Sketch lightly.

2. Sketch a slightly larger circle that over-laps halfway into one of the other circles (this will be the horse's chest area).

front   rear

3. Now, forget about the middle circle. Make a peanut shape out of the two end circles (the curves should be very slight). Sketch a dot in the middle of each circle.

slight curve down

slight curve up

front   rear

4. Measure the key distance (center of front circle to back edge of rear circle) with a pencil or a ruler.

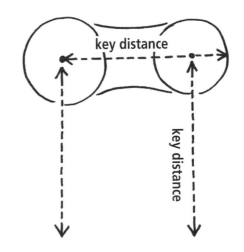

front   rear

Quick Starts Tips!™

Don't forget proportion! While you are following these steps, look at a picture or statue of a horse. Would you say the head is about as long as the chest is thick? Now look at your sketch. Are the proportions the same? By looking back and forth from the model to your drawing, you are learning to compare the real proportions and apply them to your drawing. Try not to see just the whole horse, but rather look at how the parts relate to one another.

5. Use the key distance to measure the length of the legs, going straight down from the two dots.

key distance

key distance

6. The line for the neck goes out diagonally from the front circle to the top of the head. This line is slightly shorter than the key distance. The length of the head is about half the key distance.

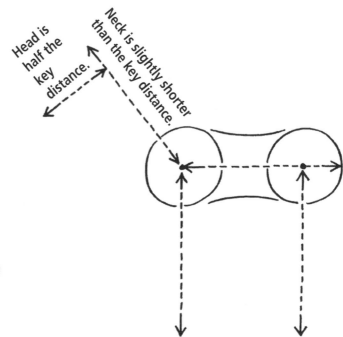

Head is half the key distance.

Neck is slightly shorter than the key distance.

7. Now that you have the proportions laid out, use basic shapes (pages 8–9) to block out the legs and the head of the horse.

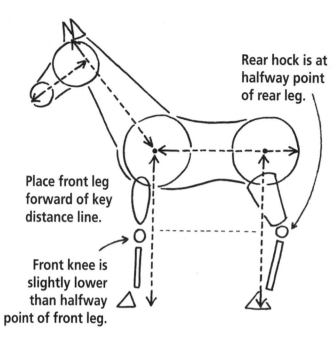

Rear hock is at halfway point of rear leg.

Place front leg forward of key distance line.

Front knee is slightly lower than halfway point of front leg.

8. Gently erase the key distance lines. Redraw the outline in pencil, still keeping it light. Sketch in some of the details like the eye, nostril, mouth, mane, and tail. Keep working lightly in pencil until you are happy with the way the drawing looks.

9. Using an ink pen, draw over just the lines and details that you want to keep. Go slowly and carefully at this step! Remember to watch where you are going with the pen.

10. Carefully and thoroughly erase all the pencil marks. Be careful not to crumple the paper.

Congratulations! You now have drawn a classic horse pose! Next, you'll see how to add more detail to your horse drawings.

chapter 2

Creating Character with Details

Are you becoming more comfortable drawing the basic, overall shape of a horse? While you continue practicing, we can begin doing some fine-tuning. By focusing on the details of your horse — the eyes, the position of the legs, the mane blowing in the wind — you can give your horse a personality and tell more of a story with your drawing. You can also have fun doing great close-ups of the head.

Adding details requires you to observe proportion, visualize shapes in each part of the horse, and, of course, practice, just as you did with the entire horse.

The Basics of Getting A-Head!

What part of the horse shows the most personality? The head! So let's start there. And can you guess how we'll start? That's right, basic shapes.

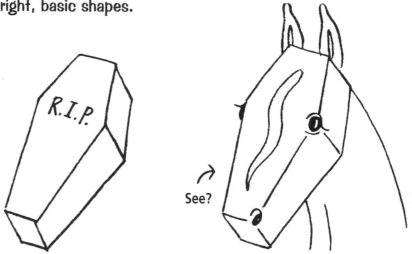

Do you know what shape an old-fashioned coffin is (like the ones in old vampire movies)? Well, believe it or not, the old vampire coffin is a very handy shape to use for sketching a horse head!

Actually, you don't have to draw a coffin shape to sketch a realistic horse head. It just helps to keep that shape in mind as you work, because a horse's head is kind of like a box — it has many sides, or *planes*. (And the coffin comes in handy when you're adding the facial features, as you will see!)

By thinking of a box, or coffin shape, you will remember to pay attention to all the planes on a horse's face. Let's "build" a head now, using basic shapes. Remember to sketch lightly in pencil!

1. Draw two circles on a diagonal line. Make the top one about twice as big as the bottom one.

2. Place the coffin shape on the top half of the diagonal line and slightly enlarge the big circle for the horse's cheek.

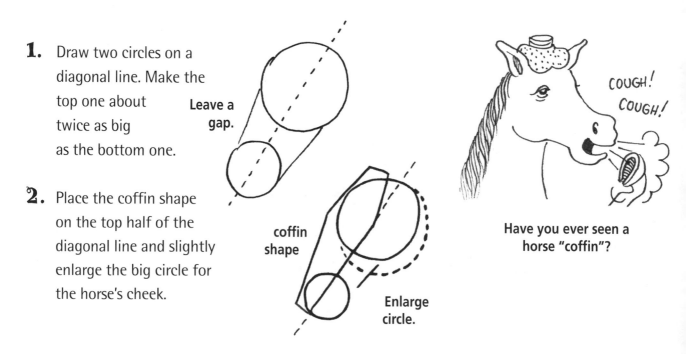

Leave a gap.

coffin shape

Enlarge circle.

Have you ever seen a horse "coffin"?

COUGH! COUGH!

3. Look at how the coffin shape can help you place the details on a horse's head!

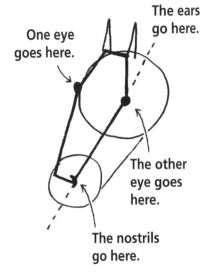

One eye goes here.

The ears go here.

The other eye goes here.

The nostrils go here.

4. Now, tilt the ears forward, and sketch a curved neck line on top, and a straight neck line on the bottom. Erase a little if you want to.

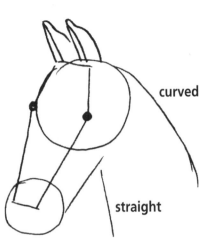

curved

straight

5. Sketch and develop all the lines — especially around the muzzle and cheek. To make the eyes, ears, nostrils, and mouth look more realistic, see pages 22–24.

muzzle

6. Using your ink pen, draw over just the lines you want to keep.

7. Finally, erase all the pencil lines carefully and admire the finished picture!

The eyes Have It!

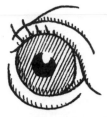

A horse's eyes show the horse's emotions, which help to give your horse a distinct character. When you're drawing a close-up of a horse's head, the eye is very important, so make it as detailed as you want, with texture (page 52), shading (page 53), and even color (page 54).

1. An eyeball is shaped like a — uh — ball, so start with a circle.

2. To make the upper eyelid, at the top of the circle draw a curved line at an angle. It should slice off the circle's top, making a small crescent moon.

    Then, sketch the lower lid at the bottom of the circle.

center line of circle

upper lid

lower lid

3. Draw a small circle for the pupil.

4. Draw a "bite" out of the top of the small circle. Then, add a curved line under the lower lid.

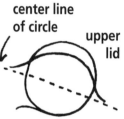

5. Ink over just the lines shown in the example. Fill in the small circle, *except* for the "bite" area. Shade or color the rest of the eye, and carefully erase all pencil marks.

Full Body? Smaller Eye!

In a full-body drawing, the eye will be much smaller and not so prominent. Here is a short-cut to a realistic small eye without too much detail.

1. Start with a curve; add a circle.

2. Add a "bite" oval and a line on the bottom that follows the curve of the circle.

3. Ink over the lines and fill in the circle — but not the "bite" oval.

  **DRAWING HORSES**

...ALL THE BETTER TO "EAR" YOU WITH!

A horse's ear is kind of a funny shape to begin with. (It reminds me of a football. What do you see?) When those ears point in different directions, they show a horse's reactions. It's fun to show a horse's responses with its ears!

See how it gets darker the deeper you go?

1. To draw a simple ear, start with a tilted football shape.

2. Make an outline around the sides and extend it to a rounded point on top.

3. Add some shading on half of the football shape (the inside of the ear).

Ears in Action

Can you match these ears with the horse's response? (Notice how the football shape is fat or skinny, depending on the position of the ear.)

1. Content
2. Mad
3. Alert

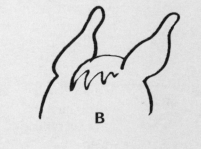

A

B

C

Answers: (1) C; (2) B; (3) A.

Nostrils and Mouth

Drawing realistic nostrils on the muzzle is easy, once you learn to use the proper shape. (Hint: it's *not* a circle!)

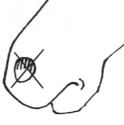

Circle

Squash!

Crookneck squash

1. Start with an oval, just to place the nostril in its correct position.

2. Change the oval into a squash shape, with the "neck" of the squash pointing forward.

3. Shade it from dark to light, with the darkest part in the fold of the nostril (the "neck" of the squash).

Look at how the shape of the nostril changes as the horse's head turns.

Three-quarter view

Front view

To draw flared nostrils, just make everything wider.

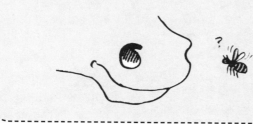

Mouth

The mouth of a horse is defined by its thick, rubbery lips. (If you've ever tried to feed a carrot to a hungry horse, you know what I mean!)

Try to draw little bulges to suggest thick lips.

GETTING A LEG UP

The "Bronc-ettes"

Front Legs

The easiest way to set up your drawing of the front leg is to work from a straight line. Notice how the entire "foot" (really the hoof and pastern) is forward of the line, with the back of the hoof just touching it.

Let's practice using a straight line and basic shapes to draw a front leg.

foreleg

knee

cannon

pastern

hoof

fetlock

1. Draw a vertical line (use a ruler if you like). Mark the midpoint.

2. Sketch some basic shapes to represent the four parts of the leg. The circle at the midpoint is for the knee. The straight line should go through the middle of the leg shapes and behind the hoof shape.

midpoint

The pastern and hoof are forward of line.

3. Trace lightly around the outsides of the shapes you made, joining them together. Notice how the angle of the pastern is parallel to the top slope of the hoof.

top slope of hoof

angle of pastern

4. Ink over just the outside lines. Gently erase the pencil marks.

Back Legs

A horse's back leg is more challenging to draw than the front, so give yourself more time to practice it. The shape and the angles of the leg can vary greatly, depending on what the horse is doing. To learn the basic shapes and angles, we'll start by drawing the back leg of a horse that is standing still, just as we did with the front leg.

See how a vertical line can also be used to set up the parts of the back leg?

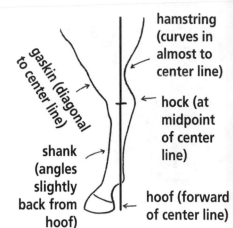

gaskin (diagonal to center line)

hamstring (curves in almost to center line)

hock (at midpoint of center line)

shank (angles slightly back from hoof)

hoof (forward of center line)

1. Draw a vertical line and mark the midpoint.

midpoint

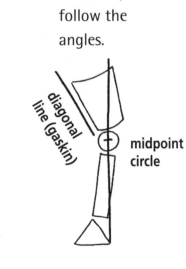

diagonal line (gaskin)

midpoint circle

2. Now place the basic shapes to follow the angles.

3. Trace lightly around the outsides of the shapes, and follow the curve of the rump down to where the hamstring area bends in — nearly to the midpoint. This will take some practice, so try it several times!

Follow the curve of rump *in* to hamstring and *out* at hock.

Curve in at pastern.

Quick Starts Tips!™

Practice the parts separately. When you practice drawing the legs and leg parts separately, you are learning their shapes and sizes in relation to each other. The more time that you spend practicing the parts, the easier it will be to draw the entire picture — and the more real your horse will look!

4. Ink over the final lines; erase pencil marks.

Hooves and Pasterns ("Ankles")

The hooves and pasterns of a horse can be more difficult to draw than they look. As with most things, however, the more you look at them and study their shapes, the easier it becomes to draw them.

Start by thinking of the shape of a horse's hoof as a triangle. Then look at all the ways it is different from a triangle. Use these observations when you use a triangle shape to sketch your rough drawings.

The actual hoof shape looks more like an electric iron.

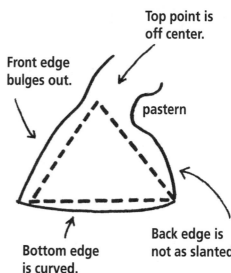

Top point is off center.

Front edge bulges out.

pastern

Back edge is not as slanted.

Bottom edge is curved.

The front edge slopes more than back edge.

The coronet (top line of hoof) slopes down from front to back.

← fetlock

← pastern

← coronet

← heel

The Hoof Area

Try sketching the hoof as if you are looking at it from different angles.

From below

From the front

From the side

Notice that when a horse bends its hoof back, the rear of the pastern looks like a horseshoe!

Manes

Drawing a basic mane is easy. For fancy mane decorations, see page 57!

The "mayne" is my favorite part of the horse. Can you guess why?

1. Make some pencil lines to show which way the mane will hang. Start with one curved line at the top, and add more lines that curve the same way.

2. The finished drawing of the mane will look more real if the lines you draw are somewhat unevenly spaced and of different lengths.

3. The *forelock* (the part of a mane growing between a horse's ears) looks a lot like a tail.

To draw a mane that's blowing in the wind, start with one strand of hair that is lifted off the neck. (It looks better if the mane is longer.) Then, add more curved lines, blowing in different groups.

All it takes are some curved, pointed lines that look like claws.

Tails

Drawing the tail in different positions adds expression or character to the horse in your drawing. For most side-view poses, it looks more realistic to separate the tail from the body just a little bit (at the *dock* area).

dock

You don't have to draw every hair in the tail to make it look realistic!

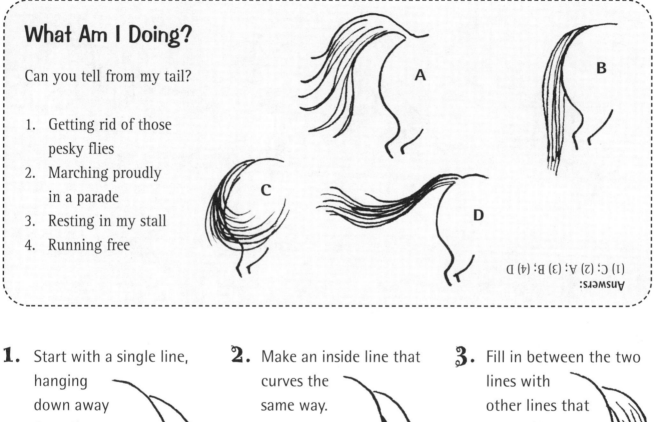

What Am I Doing?

Can you tell from my tail?

1. Getting rid of those pesky flies
2. Marching proudly in a parade
3. Resting in my stall
4. Running free

A

B

C

D

Answers: (1) C; (2) A; (3) B; (4) D

1. Start with a single line, hanging down away from the rump.

line 1

2. Make an inside line that curves the same way.

line 2   line 1

3. Fill in between the two lines with other lines that curve the same way. Some should be long, and some should be short. (It's OK if they touch.)

Different Horse Breeds

Clydesdale

Everything is big on a Clydesdale! Big head, thick neck, massive shoulders, even a big rump (make the rear body circle bigger). Of course, it also has those characteristic hairy feet, which makes things easier if you have trouble drawing hooves!

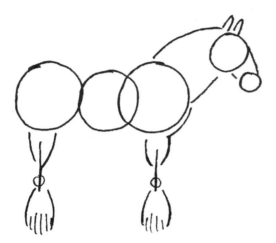

Arabian

The Arabian is a slender, high-spirited breed. You can show this by making the chest and neck a little thinner. The face has a slight curve to the front, resulting in a slim muzzle. The legs are slender and graceful. Draw it with its head and tail held high!

chapter 3

Horses in Motion: Poses and Gaits

You've probably noticed that horses don't stand around posed like perfect statues. So while that basic position (page 16) is a good way to start drawing them, soon you'll want to move on to other positions. We'll begin again with the side view because it's the easiest angle to learn, and then we'll try some different angles.

After that, I'll help you to capture the look of a horse on the move. Whether it's simply trotting or flying over a jump, a moving horse is "poetry in motion." If you're patient and take the time to observe how the basic shapes move in proportion to one another, you'll be able to draw some nice horse "poems."

Different Side Positions

Look at side views of horses in different poses. Try to visualize where the basic shapes will go when the horses are in those positions. Practice drawing those poses until you become comfortable with the way the proportions and key distances (page 15) always stay the same, while the basic shapes move and overlap each other. You can always trace (page 9) them first if you like.

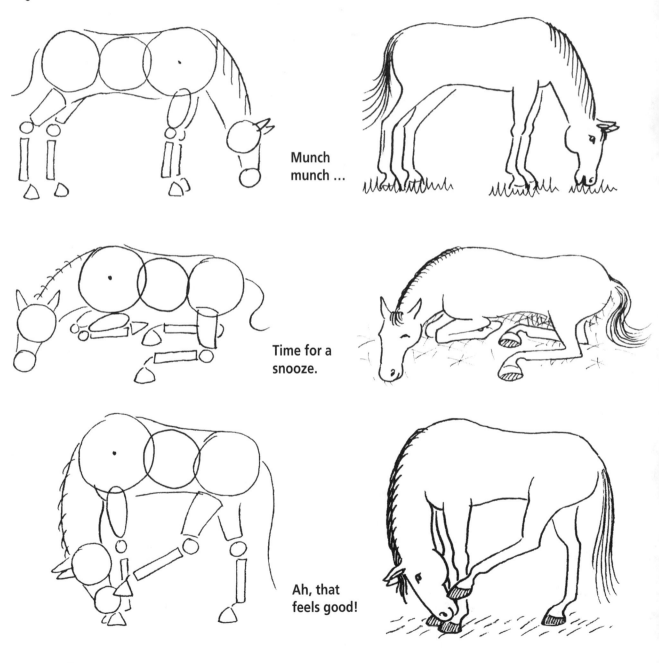

Munch munch ...

Time for a snooze.

Ah, that feels good!

DRAWING THE HORSE FROM DIFFERENT ANGLES

When a horse's body moves, the basic shapes inside its body move, too. Remember the three body circles (that turn into two) when you're sketching the body (pages 8–9)? Using those two circles to position the horse is the secret to drawing the horse from different angles.

Think of two oranges on a plate.

When you turn the plate, one orange appears to move in front of the other.

Well, the same thing happens when you turn a horse! From the front or the back, you'll see the two circles overlap.

No matter what angle you want to draw, start by figuring out how the circles will be positioned!

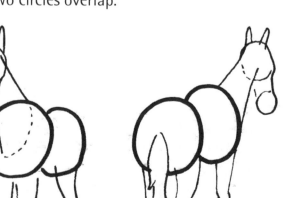

Different Head Angles

Drawing a horse's head at different angles is just like drawing the body — think of the basic shapes *first* and how they will turn as the horse's head turns. Study these shapes and their proportions.

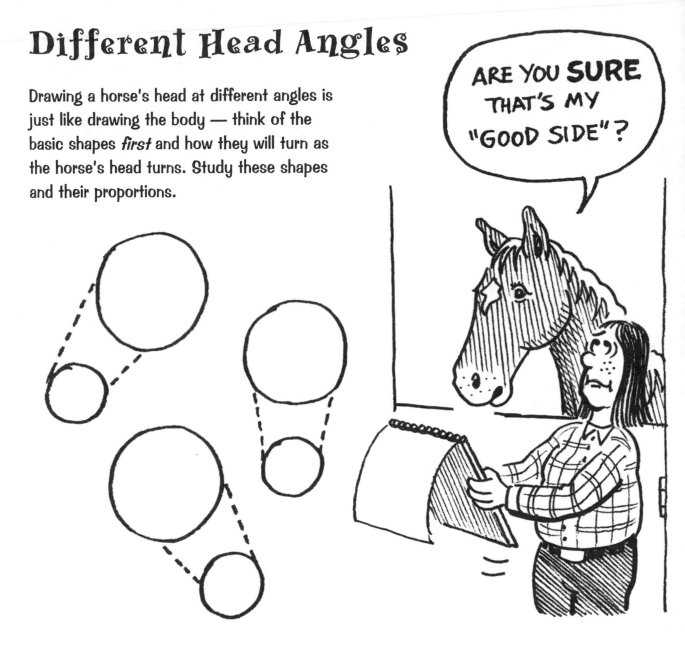

ARE YOU **SURE** THAT'S MY "GOOD SIDE"?

Here are the two important things to remember for most head positions:

- The big circle is about twice as big as the small circle for the muzzle.
- The distance between the circles is about half the size of the small circle.

Front View

1. Look back at the side view of the horse's head (page 20). Can you see the coffin shape?

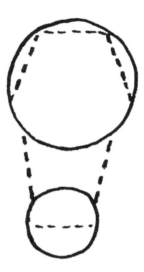

Bring the two lines from the big circle to the small circle in just a little.

2. Sketch two crossing lines in the big circle to help place the eye, ear, and neck lines. The nostrils and mouth go in the small circle.

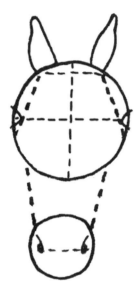

3. Add other features to finish the face. Erase the circle lines that you don't need.

Other Head Positions

Again, think of the two circles as shapes that can move as the head moves.

In some head positions, they overlap each other.

The last thing a carrot sees!

GIDDYUP!
DRAWING DIFFERENT GAITS

The ways that a horse positions its legs and feet to move at different speeds are called *gaits*. Accurate leg positions (with the shapes in proportion to one another!) are the keys to making a realistic drawing of a horse moving at different gaits.

You might want to trace these gaits, from slowest (walking) to fastest (galloping) to get some practice before you sketch without tracing. (Enlarge on a photocopier for larger shapes to work on.) To help you see the leg positions, I have shaded the legs on the far side of the horse. (You don't have to shade the legs this way in your drawings.) Then see pages 38–39 for a step-by-step look at how to sketch all four legs in motion.

Walking

A horse walks by picking up and putting down each hoof separately. This means that there are almost always three hooves on the ground.

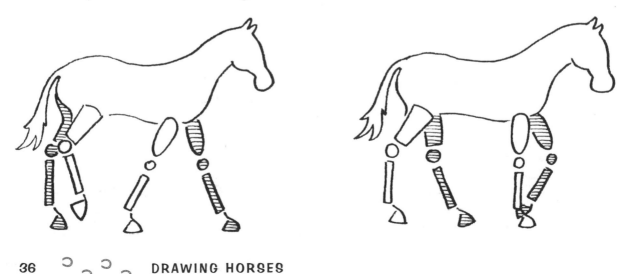

Trotting

In this gait, the horse moves its diagonal legs together. Look for positions that show this trait.

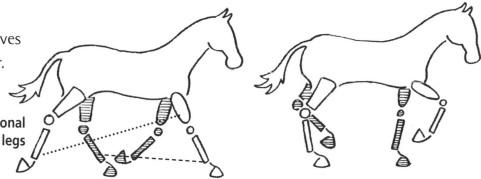

diagonal legs

Cantering

This is a three-beat gait, but there may be times when all four hooves are off the ground.

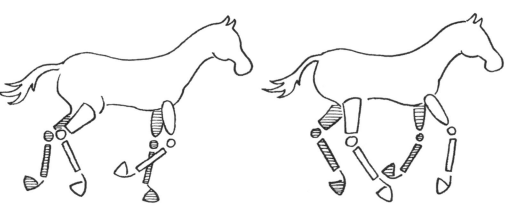

Galloping

This is the fastest gait, so the horse is really stretched out and pushing forward.

On the Move!

Notice how in the faster gaits, the horse's neck is stretched out, and the head points forward more. Also, its weight seems to push forward. Do you see any other differences?

Quick Starts Tips!™

Hold that pose! You don't have to limit yourself to these poses to show a horse in motion. Watch your favorite horse movie on video or DVD. Pause it when you see a gait you want to draw and study the still picture you see. It's much easier to draw a horse that's standing still!

Drawing Four Moving Legs

Let's take a closer look at how to sketch the legs of a trotting horse. Drawing all four individual legs together is just the way it sounds — you'll draw each leg separately, but you'll try to make them look as if they are working together. So, you'll be more successful if you do a series of three or four rough sketches to get the length and position of each leg and how they relate to one another just right. You can use the same step-by-step method for other leg positions. Don't worry about drawing perfect legs at this stage — it's just a practice sketch!

1. Use short lines and circles to show where the joints are (see pages 25–26 to review the differences in proportion between the front and the rear legs, if you need to). Make sure that the joints closest to the horse's body (I'll call them all "knees" here) are all about the same distance away from the horse's body.

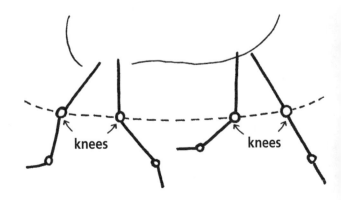

knees   knees

2. Lightly sketch the basic shapes that make up each leg. The jointed lines should go through the middle of all the shapes. Remember to leave small spaces between the shapes and the joints.

See how the triangle shapes for the hooves are slightly slanted? This helps to show that the horse is in motion.

3. Now, sketch lightly around the edges of the shapes, using them as a guide to help you form the legs. Pay attention to details like the roundness of the "knees" and which legs might overlap others. Erase and redraw as needed, until you like the way it looks.

4. Finally, ink carefully over the lines you want to keep. Again, pay attention to which legs might overlap others. Gently erase all the pencil marks to reveal your beautiful drawing that you did with no trouble at all!

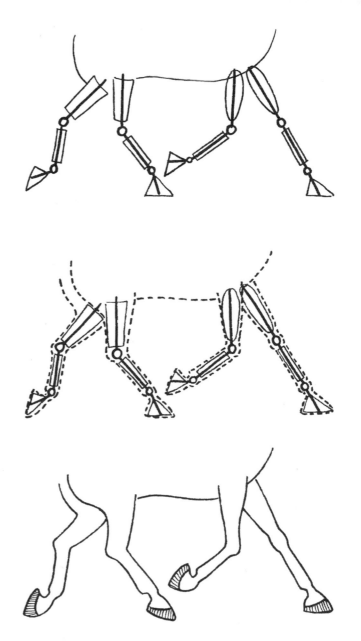

✎ *Quick Starts Tips!*™

Ready to skip some steps? These detailed steps are so you can learn the proper technique and then practice it. As you get more confident in your drawing ability, you will probably skip some of these steps. And that's OK — in fact, it's great!

A jumping horse is a beautiful, awesome thing to watch. It makes a beautiful drawing, too! To start, let's look at how the proportions of the horse's body change during a jump.

The Stages of a Jump

A horse stretches out its body when it's jumping. So that your drawing looks more realistic, stretch out the circles of the body when you sketch them. This makes the horse's back look longer and more graceful as it jumps.

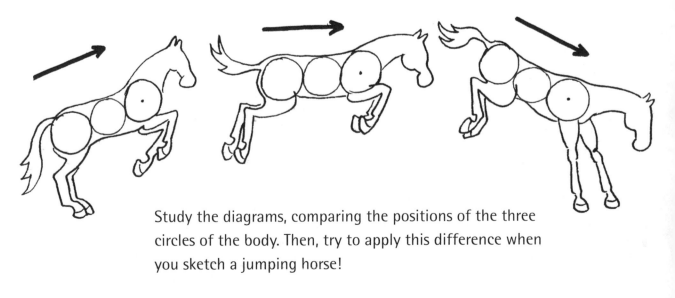

Study the diagrams, comparing the positions of the three circles of the body. Then, try to apply this difference when you sketch a jumping horse!

Here's a horse going up over the jump and then coming down on the other side.
I have shown you the basic shapes, followed by a finished drawing. Now you
know how to use the in-between steps from the Classic Horse-Statue pose
(pages 16–18) and the **R.I.D.E.** technique (pages 10–12) to clear that
jump easily and ride off with a beautiful series of finished drawings!

chapter 4

Foals and Ponies

What could possibly be more adorable than a baby horse, called a *foal*? Many of the horse-drawing secrets you've already learned will help you draw a foal, too. But it's also important to look closely at all the ways a foal differs from an adult horse (and there are many). Close attention to these details will make your drawing that much more realistic.

"JUNIOR"

Getting to Know "Junior"

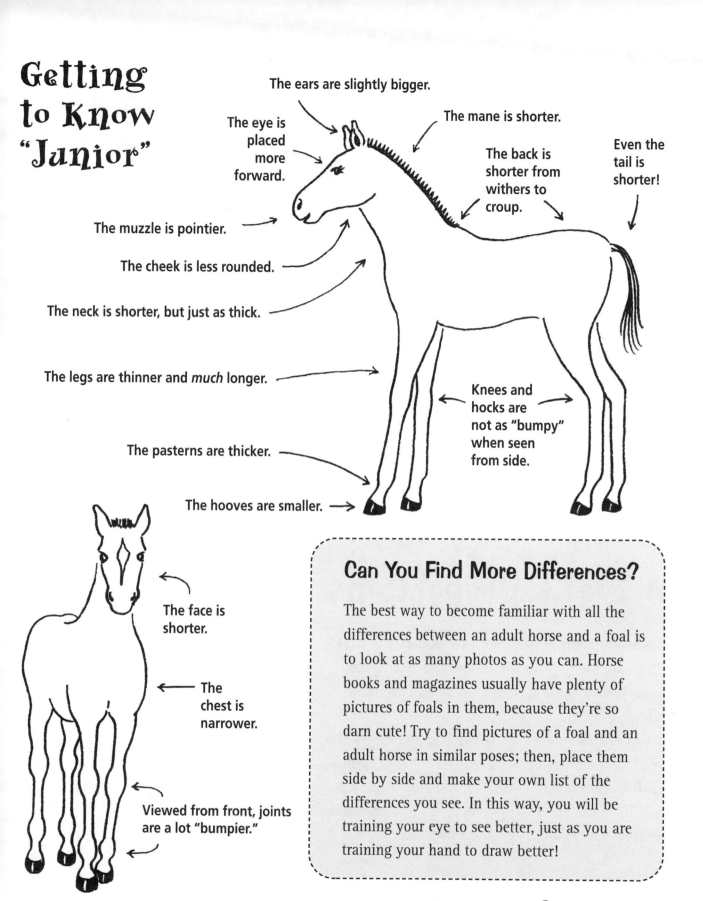

The ears are slightly bigger.

The mane is shorter.

The eye is placed more forward.

The back is shorter from withers to croup.

Even the tail is shorter!

The muzzle is pointier.

The cheek is less rounded.

The neck is shorter, but just as thick.

The legs are thinner and *much* longer.

Knees and hocks are not as "bumpy" when seen from side.

The pasterns are thicker.

The hooves are smaller.

The face is shorter.

The chest is narrower.

Viewed from front, joints are a lot "bumpier."

Can You Find More Differences?

The best way to become familiar with all the differences between an adult horse and a foal is to look at as many photos as you can. Horse books and magazines usually have plenty of pictures of foals in them, because they're so darn cute! Try to find pictures of a foal and an adult horse in similar poses; then, place them side by side and make your own list of the differences you see. In this way, you will be training your eye to see better, just as you are training your hand to draw better!

A Foal's Proportions

Foals are baby horses, so their bodies still have to grow. Many proportions are different! Take time to study the differences to improve your drawing.

Remember the key distance (page 15) — the measurement you use to lay out the proportions of the adult horse's body? It's a little bit different for a foal. But the handy R.I.D.E. technique (pages 10–12) works just the same way!

Foal Facts

A female foal is often called a *filly*, while a male foal is known as a *colt*. This fact doesn't make any difference when you draw them, but sometimes it's fun to add a bow or another prop to show your foal as a boy or a girl.

Here's how to set up a foal's proportions.

1. Draw two circles of the same size that just touch each other. These can be any size, depending on how big your drawing will be.

2. Make a slightly bigger circle for the chest. The left edge of the middle circle should cut through the middle of the bigger circle. Mark A, B, and C to show the key distances.

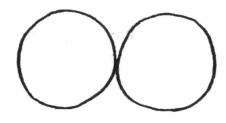

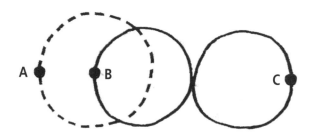

3. Measure the proportions for legs, neck, and head.

4. The circles for the head should be closer together than for an adult horse. Sketch the neck lines almost as wide as the chest, curving on the top. Place the ears at the top of the center neck line.

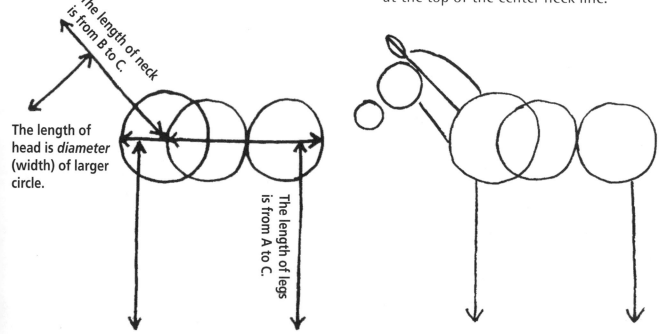

The length of neck is from B to C.

The length of head is *diameter* (width) of larger circle.

The length of legs is from A to C.

5. Add the basic shapes for the front and rear legs. Make the legs thinner than for an adult horse. Keep the hooves small and right on the vertical leg lines.

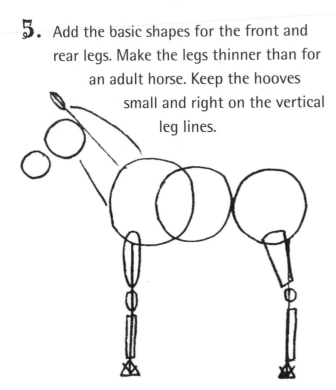

6. Make a rough sketch around the outside of all the shapes, improving the shape of the foal. Add face details, a mane, and a tail. Add a second pair of legs.

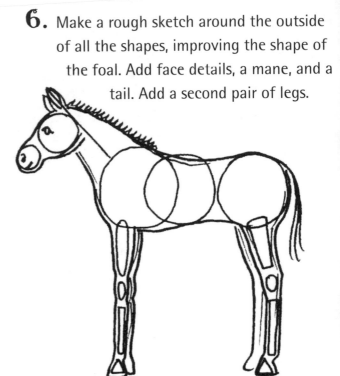

7. When you are happy with your rough pencil sketch, draw carefully over the lines you want to keep in ink. Take your time at this step!

8. After the ink dries, carefully erase all the pencil marks, and add any final details that you want. Now you have a nice, clean drawing of a cute little foal, ready to add texture (page 52), shading (page 53), or color (page 54)!

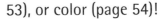

FOALS IN MOTION

Foals are very playful, so try to sketch them in positions that show their fun personalities! You can use all the action poses and gaits you learned in the previous chapter (pages 31–41). Here are some frisky foals you can draw using the R.I.D.E. technique!

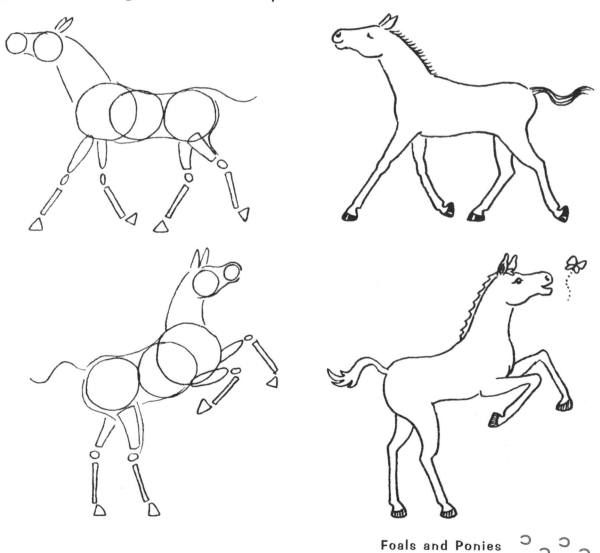

Foals and Mares

Now that you can draw real-looking baby horses *and* adults, you can draw foals *with* their moms! These drawings would look really nice with shading (page 53) and backgrounds (pages 58–61); I've left them simple so you can see how they're drawn.

When drawing mares and foals together, try to show how mom and baby might feel about each other.

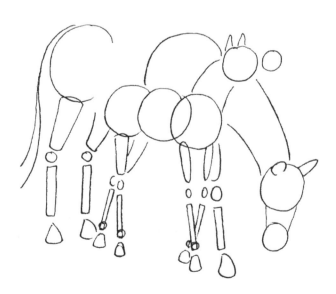

You don't need to draw all the details to make a nice picture. How many legs do you see? Can you find any other shortcuts?

Quick Starts Tips!™

Don't forget the thumbnail sketch.

A thumbnail sketch (page 11) is particularly helpful when you have two overlapping figures, like a mare and a foal, in your drawing.

NO, THIS IS **NOT** WHAT I MEAN BY A "THUMBNAIL SKETCH"!

It's OK to sketch the shapes overlapping when you do it "thumbnail style." Actually, that's the whole point, so you can practice how the shapes will overlap when you set up your final drawing.

Ponies

Ponies (small horses) have a long body, a short, thick neck, and very short legs. Use three circles for the body, and make the legs a little longer than the body is thick.

chapter 5

Finishing Touches

Wow! Your horse drawings are impressive now! If you want to add shading, color, pieces of tack (like a saddle or a bridle), or if you want to place your horses in a scene, I'll show you more of the tricks and techniques that I know.

CAN YOU DRAW ME WITH ONE OF THOSE FANCY, NEW BRIDLES?

Oh, What a Few More Lines Will Do!

Adding a few details to your drawings can make them look even more realistic. This picture shows just a few examples.

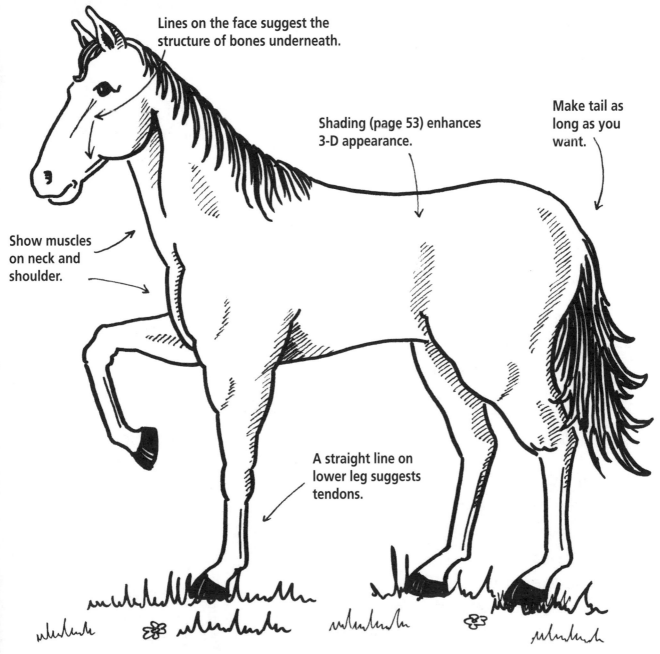

Lines on the face suggest the structure of bones underneath.

Shading (page 53) enhances 3-D appearance.

Make tail as long as you want.

Show muscles on neck and shoulder.

A straight line on lower leg suggests tendons.

Squiggly lines suggest a grassy field. For a more detailed background, see pages 58–61.

TEXTURE

Use texture (like hair) to add some fantastic effects to your drawings. I've got to tell you — it does take patience!

Drawing Texture (with Ink Pens)

Tiny dots. Using a felt-tip pen with a fine tip, make hundreds of dots on your horse, all about the same distance apart. For darker areas, make the dots closer together. This takes a lot of patience, but it's hard to mess it up!

Horse hairs. Also using a fine tip, make hundreds of short dashes, about the same distance apart. You can make them closer together to show shading (page 53). Try to make the hairs follow the curves of the horse — and keep them short!

Hatch marks. Make rows of longer lines, evenly spaced and following the contours of the horse wherever possible. Make crosshatch marks where you want shading.

Rubbing Texture
(with pencil or colored pencil)

With this method, you rub gently with a pencil. Place the drawing on top of a textured surface. When you rub with your pencil, that texture will be transferred to your picture!

Here are some materials that make interesting textures for a horse: wood grain, rough tile, sandpaper, tablecloth, and textured wallpaper.

Quick Starts Tips!™

Start on scrap paper. Practice these textures using ink pens or rubbing texture with pencils on a separate piece of paper *first* — before you try them on a finished drawing.

SHADING

Shading is a great way to make a horse drawing look more realistic by giving it a three-dimensional effect. Plus, it's just plain fun to do!

Here's the secret to shading — choose the direction that the light is coming from, and shade everything *on the other side!*

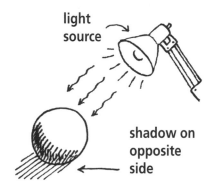

light source

shadow on opposite side

Here is an ordinary, unshaded horse.

Choose a light source; then, decide where the shadows should go, based on the shape of the horse. Remember that even with the shape of the head, some areas will cast a shadow.

Combine texture (page 52) and shading effects for a really cool look!

Shading can show the muscles on a horse, the curve of its body, and other details like the insides of ears and nostrils (*eeew!*). Including the horse's shadow in your drawing will always make it more realistic, because it will look as if the horse is really standing on the ground.

WHERE DO YOU THINK THE SUN IS?

Using Color

Adding color is a great way to make your horse drawing look more authentic. You have to be careful, however — the wrong colors or the wrong kinds of pens can ruin a drawing or make it look *un*natural.

I recommend using colored pencils, because you can take your time and build up the color, which you can't always do with felt-tip pens. Colored pencils are also great for adding texture and shading to the drawing to make it look even more realistic!

Adding Color

- Add color last — after you've made all your pencil improvements, outlined the final lines in ink, and erased all the pencil marks.

- If you have a nice drawing in ink, and you are worried about ruining it with color, make some photocopies of it first and color the copies instead of your original ink drawing.

- Try your colors and coloring techniques on a piece of scrap paper first — *before* you experiment with them on your completed drawing. Most colors can't be erased.

- It's easy to make the color darker, but very difficult to make it lighter! So, when using colored pencils, first fill in the areas to be colored very lightly, and go over it again and again in places where you want darker color.

The overlapping hatch marks represent layers of colored pencil. You can use the same overlapping technique if you're shading in black and white, too!

The Tack Room

If you want to draw a picture of a horse that's "tacked up" (wearing its bridle and saddle), plan those details as part of your pencil sketch, so you can be sure it looks right before you ink over it.

Saddles

Even objects like saddles are made of basic shapes. When sketching basic shapes for objects, don't worry too much about the details like the stitching. Remember, these details might not show on a full-body picture of a horse, anyway!

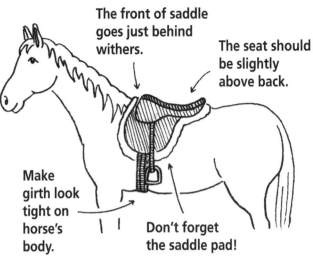

The front of saddle goes just behind withers.

The seat should be slightly above back.

Make girth look tight on horse's body.

Don't forget the saddle pad!

English saddle

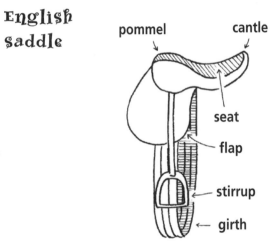

pommel

cantle

seat

flap

stirrup

girth

Western saddle

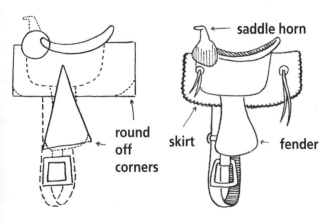

saddle horn

round off corners

skirt

fender

A Horse Blanket

The blanket covers the horse's body, so it's easy to draw a blanket by covering the basic shapes that make up the body.

Start with the circles, sketch the blanket over them, then add the parts of the body not covered by the blanket.

Bridles, Reins, and Halters

Bridles, reins, and halters are much more than just lines drawn on a horse's head. Here are some handy tips to make the tack look as if the horse is really wearing it.

Parts of a Bridle

Study the parts of a bridle, so you can draw them all in their proper places.

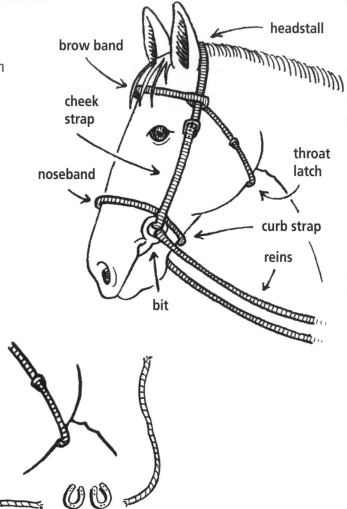

brow band

headstall

cheek strap

throat latch

noseband

curb strap

reins

bit

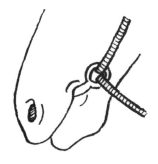

Quick Starts Tips!™

Drawing 3-D curves. To draw a strap that appears to go around something, think of it as two lines, instead of just one. See how the throat latch seems to curve around the edge of the horse's face?

Here's a close-up look at a bridle connection. Try to stretch the corners of the horse's mouth around the bit, to show its roundness, and how it's pulling back on the mouth.

Snaffle bit

Curb bit

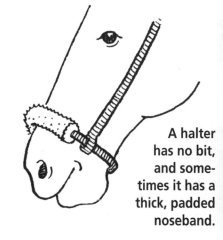

A halter has no bit, and sometimes it has a thick, padded noseband.

MANE DECORATIONS

One of the nicest things about drawing your own horses is that you can braid the mane or decorate it just about any way that you want — and it's easy to get the horse to stand still!

It's Show Time!

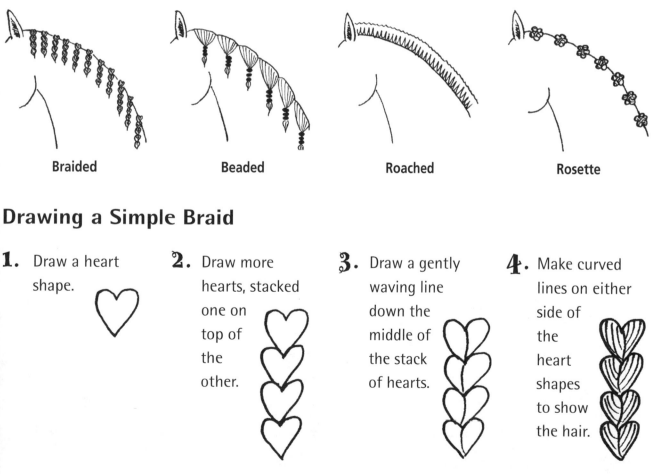

Braided **Beaded** **Roached** **Rosette**

Drawing a Simple Braid

1. Draw a heart shape.

2. Draw more hearts, stacked one on top of the other.

3. Draw a gently waving line down the middle of the stack of hearts.

4. Make curved lines on either side of the heart shapes to show the hair.

Backgrounds and Scenery

Well, now you know how to draw a realistic-looking horse. If you decide to add a barn, a corral, or natural settings like mountains and pastures, you'll want them to look natural, too.

Here are my two methods for adding background scenery so that the result is a final drawing that's as good as your horse!

Use the horse as a ruler to size the other objects in the picture.

If you want to add something like a barn or a fence to your drawing, you need to have it the right size.

To match the size of objects with the size of a horse, just use the horse as a ruler! A horse's height is measured from the ground to its withers ("shoulders"). Every object has a size in relation to a horse:

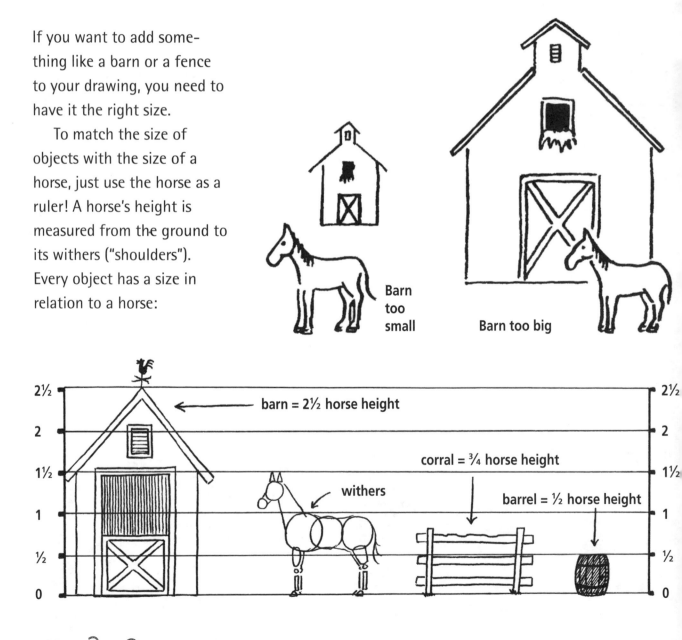

Barn too small

Barn too big

barn = 2½ horse height

corral = ¾ horse height

withers

barrel = ½ horse height

2½   2   1½   1   ½   0

And now, here's my *final* horse-drawing secret — my foolproof method for getting both the horse drawing and the background just the way you want it:

Draw the horse and background separately; then put the two drawings together.

If everything else in your picture will be behind the horse, draw your background and other objects on a separate piece of paper, until they look the way you want. (Don't forget to use the R.I.D.E. technique, pages 10–12, for the background to make it look just right!) This way, you won't ruin a finished horse picture that you like with a background that you're not happy with. Then, *merge* the two drawings by tracing!

Let's look at this technique in more detail.

1. Line up the edges of a blank piece of paper, so it fits perfectly over your horse drawing.

Put the tape on the blank paper only, but so that it holds *both* pieces of paper in place.

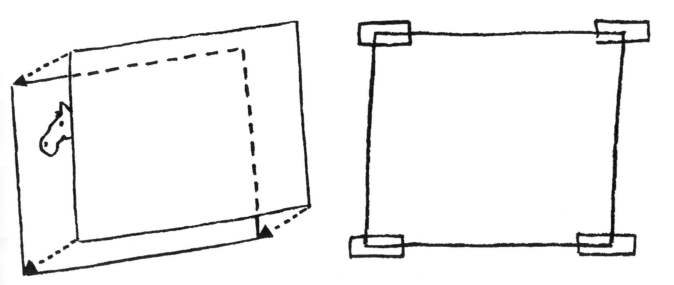

2. Sketch a rough outline of your horse drawing onto the blank paper, by tracing over the lines that you can see through the paper. Don't worry too much about making a "perfect" sketch. You're just trying to mark the position of the horse on the blank paper. Now, separate the two pieces of paper.

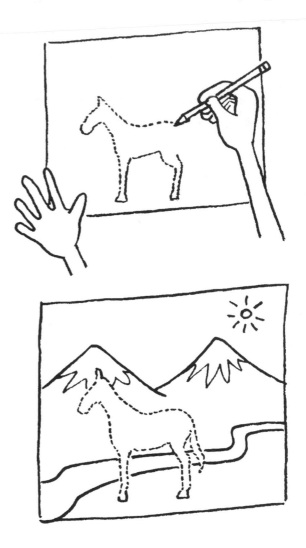

3. Sketch your background *around* the traced outline of the horse. When you like the way it looks, ink over the pencil lines.

You don't need to erase pencil marks or add final details. This step is just to blend the background with the position of the horse.

If you don't like the background picture, just start over at step 1 again, until you get just what you want.

Quick Starts Tips!™

Window tracing. An easy way to trace is to tape your drawing to a bright window and put another piece of paper over it. Be careful not to lean too hard!

4. Now, switch the papers around, so that the background sketch is on the bottom, and the finished horse picture is on the top. Then, lightly trace your background picture onto your horse picture.

Use the R.I.D.E. technique to finish the drawing, fine-tuning the details of the background and then inking over the final lines.

Ta-da! What a great-looking drawing!

I hope you have found this book as much fun to read and learn from as it was for me to draw! If you keep practicing my tips and techniques, I know your drawings will improve dramatically. Someday I hope to see one of your horse pictures in a museum!

I'M GOING TO BE FAMOUS!

The Horse from Forelock to Fetlock

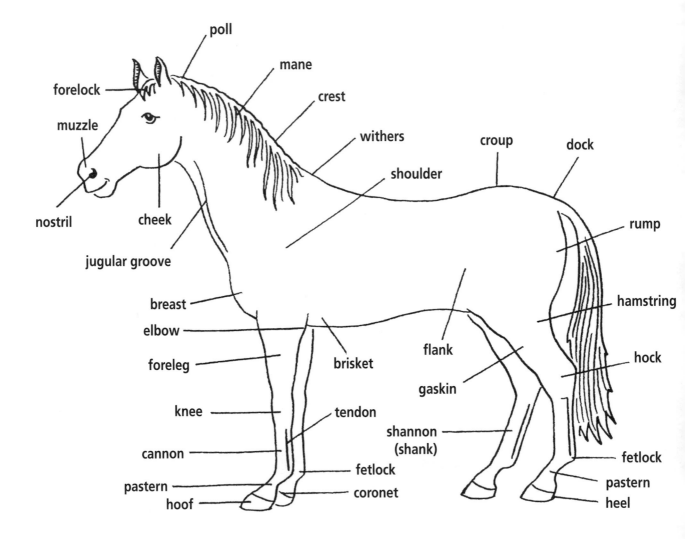

poll

mane

crest

forelock

muzzle

withers

croup

dock

nostril

cheek

shoulder

rump

jugular groove

breast

hamstring

elbow

foreleg

flank

hock

brisket

knee

gaskin

tendon

cannon

shannon
(shank)

fetlock

pastern

fetlock

pastern

hoof

coronet

heel

Index

More good books from *Williamson Publishing*
Please see below for ordering information or to visit our website. Thank you.

Quick Starts for Kids!™ books for ages 8 to adult
are each 64 pages, fully illustrated, trade paper, 8 x 10, $7.95 US/$10.95 CAN.

Also by Don Mayne:
Oppenheim Toy Portfolio Gold Award
DRAW YOUR OWN CARTOONS!

40 KNOTS TO KNOW
Hitches, Loops, Bends & Bindings
by Emily Stetson

Dr. Toy 10 Best Socially Responsible Products
Dr. Toy 100 Best Children's Products
MAKE YOUR OWN BIRDHOUSES & FEEDERS
by Robyn Haus

GARDEN FUN!
Indoors & Out; In Pots & Small Spots
by Vicky Congdon

Parents' Choice Approved
BAKE THE BEST-EVER COOKIES!
by Sarah A. Williamson

BE A CLOWN!
Techniques from a Real Clown
by Ron Burgess

YO-YO!
Tips & Tricks from a Pro
by Ron Burgess

MAKE YOUR OWN CHRISTMAS ORNAMENTS
by Ginger Johnson

REALLY COOL FELT CRAFTS
by Peg Blanchette & Terri Thibault

MAKE YOUR OWN FUN PICTURE FRAMES!
by Matt Phillips

KIDS' EASY KNITTING PROJECTS
by Peg Blanchette

KIDS' EASY QUILTING PROJECTS
by Terri Thibault

MAKE YOUR OWN HAIRWEAR
Beaded Barrettes, Clips, Dangles & Headbands
by Diane Bazker

American Bookseller Pick of the Lists
MAKE YOUR OWN TEDDY BEARS & BEAR CLOTHES
by Sue Mahren

And more ...

Williamson's *Kids Can!*® books for ages 7 to 14
are each 144 to 176 pages, fully illustrated, trade paper,
11 x 8$^1/_2$, $12.95 US/$19.95 CAN.

Parents' Choice Recommended
KIDS' ART WORKS!
Creating with Color, Design, Texture & More
by Sandi Henry

Benjamin Franklin Best Education/Teaching Gold
Award
Parent's Guide Children's Media Award
HAND-PRINT ANIMAL ART
by Carolyn Carreiro

Parents' Choice Gold Award
American Bookseller Pick of the Lists
THE KIDS' MULTICULTURAL ART BOOK
Art & Craft Experiences from Around the World
by Alexandra M. Terzian

Visit Our Website!
www.williamsonbooks.com

To Order Books

We accept Visa and MasterCard (please include the number and expiration date). Toll-free phone orders with credit cards:

1-800-234-8791

Or, send a check with your order to:

Williamson Publishing Company
P.O. Box 185
Charlotte, Vermont 05445

Catalog request: mail, phone, or e-mail
<info@williamsonbooks.com>

Please add $4.00 for postage for one book plus $1.00 for each additional book. Satisfaction is guaranteed or full refund without questions or quibbles.